Rough Riding Reformer
THEODORE ROOSEVELT

by Gary L. Blackwood

BENCHMARK **B**OOKS

MARSHALL CAVENDISH
NEW YORK

Benchmark Books
Marshall Cavendish Corporation
99 White Plains Road
Tarrytown, New York 10591

© 1998 by Marshall Cavendish Corporation

Library of Congress Cataloging-in-Publication Data
Blackwood, Gary L.
Rough riding reformer : Theodore Roosevelt / Gary L. Blackwood.
p.   cm. — (Benchmark biographies)
Summary: Presents the life story of our twenty-sixth president, covering his illness-plagued childhood
as well as his careers as a rancher, soldier, and political reformer.
ISBN 0-7614-0520-8 (lib. bdg.)
1. Roosevelt, Theodore, 1858-1919—Juvenile literature. 2. Presidents—United States—Biography—
Juvenile literature. [1. Roosevelt, Theodore, 1858-1919. 2. Presidents.] I. Title. II. Series.
E757.B646   1998   973.91'1'092—dc21   [B]   96-53087   CIP   AC

Photo research by Debbie Needleman

Photo Credits

Front cover, pages 6 (left and center), 32, 35, 39: Archive Photos; back cover, pages 14, 19, 29, 31, 36,
38, 40, 41, 42: Corbis-Bettmann; page 4: National Portrait Gallery, Smithsonian Institution/Art
Resource, NY; pages 6 (right), 8, 9 (right), 11: Theodore Roosevelt Birthplace, National Historic Site;
page 9 (left): Sagamore Hill National Historic Site; page 12: Theodore Roosevelt Collection, Harvard
College Library by permission of the Houghton Library, Harvard University; pages 15, 16, 24, 37:
Theodore Roosevelt Collection, Harvard College Library; page 21: White House Historical Association;
page 22: Underwood & Underwood/Corbis-Bettmann; page 26: The Picture Cube/Ed Carlin; page 27:
North Wind Picture Archives.

Printed in Hong Kong

1   3   5   7   8   6   4   2

CONTENTS

President Theodore Roosevelt

BAD NEWS FROM BUFFALO

Theodore Roosevelt was hiking down a mountain when he got the news. It was a scene he'd played out twice before. When his father died, and again when his wife lay dying, he'd been gone from home. He had never forgiven himself.

Now it was President McKinley who was dying, from an assassin's bullet. Theodore hurried to his camp and hired a wagon and driver to take him to the train station. It was a hair-raising forty-mile drive. The wagon bounded over the twisting mountain road in the dark. Theodore kept ordering the driver to go faster.

At the train, a telegram was waiting. President McKinley was dead. Theodore, his vice president, was now the twenty-sixth president of the United States—at forty-two, the youngest in history. And he became one of the greatest.

But he didn't just have greatness thrust upon him. He earned it. He never saw himself as a genius. He was, he said, an ordinary man with average abilities. What made him a success was the fact that he worked so hard to develop those abilities.

*Teedie at eighteen months old.
In the 1800s, boys wore dresses until
the age of three or four.*

*At five, Teedie is now
wearing trousers.*

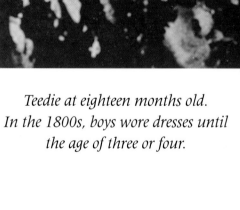

*A slightly older Teedie, still just as
serious and frail-looking*

BAD NEWS FROM BUFFALO

Theodore Roosevelt was hiking down a mountain when he got the news. It was a scene he'd played out twice before. When his father died, and again when his wife lay dying, he'd been gone from home. He had never forgiven himself.

Now it was President McKinley who was dying, from an assassin's bullet. Theodore hurried to his camp and hired a wagon and driver to take him to the train station. It was a hair-raising forty-mile drive. The wagon bounded over the twisting mountain road in the dark. Theodore kept ordering the driver to go faster.

At the train, a telegram was waiting. President McKinley was dead. Theodore, his vice president, was now the twenty-sixth president of the United States—at forty-two, the youngest in history. And he became one of the greatest.

But he didn't just have greatness thrust upon him. He earned it. He never saw himself as a genius. He was, he said, an ordinary man with average abilities. What made him a success was the fact that he worked so hard to develop those abilities.

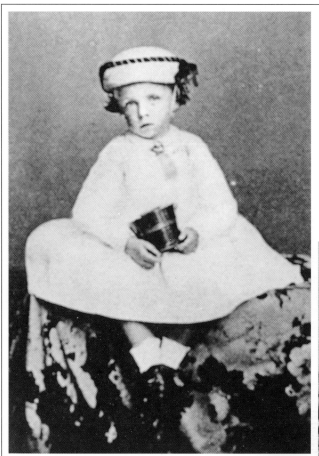

At five, Teedie is now
wearing trousers.

Teedie at eighteen months old.
In the 1800s, boys wore dresses until
the age of three or four.

A slightly older Teedie, still just as
serious and frail-looking

TEEDIE

Theodore Roosevelt was born on October 27, 1858. As a child, he showed few signs of becoming great or successful. In fact, he later wrote, "nobody seemed to think I would live."

Teedie, as the family called him, was a weak, sickly child. He had terrible headaches, nightmares, stomachaches, and attacks of asthma that made him gasp for breath like a fish out of water.

The Roosevelts were a rich New York family, and could afford the best doctors. But even the best doctors knew little about treating asthma. All the family could do was prop Teedie up and rub his chest to help him breathe. If the asthma was worse than usual, Teedie's father gave him a cup of strong coffee, or a dose of syrup that made him throw up. Sometimes he even made Teedie smoke a cigar! Other times he put his son into a carriage and galloped through the streets, to force the cold night air into Teedie's straining lungs.

The New York City house where Teedie spent his early years; later, the family moved to a larger, grander home.

BOOKS AND BEASTS

Teedie's mother nursed him patiently and kept a good sense of humor. But his father was the most important figure in his life. Teedie once wrote in his diary, "He was everything to me: father, companion, friend." Mr. Roosevelt spent much of his time raising money for charities such as the Children's Aid Society and the Newsboys' Lodging House. Yet he was never too busy to give love and attention to his children.

Teedie's younger brother, Elliott, was bright and healthy, but his sisters weren't strong. His older sister, Anna, had a crooked back. For several years

Theodore Roosevelt, Sr., was the center of his son's world. Teedie called him "Greatheart."

Teedie's mother, Martha, known to her friends as "Mittie," was considered one of New York City's most beautiful women.

doctors made her wear a steel brace. His younger sister, Corinne, had asthma attacks. But she didn't have them nearly as often or as badly as Teedie.

Because their parents worried about their health, the Roosevelt children didn't go to school. Tutors taught them at home. Bored with the narrow limits of his life, Teedie found a bigger world in books. His favorites were James Fenimore Cooper's adventure tales and the novels of Captain Mayne Reid. He longed to be like the heroes in those books, strong and courageous.

He also loved books about nature. But the real thing was even better. He returned from every outing in the country with "hedgehogs and other small beasts and reptiles, which persisted in escaping." One night at the dinner table, a mouse he'd caught startled the family by poking its head out of a large cheese.

Teedie took over a bookcase and turned it into the "Roosevelt Museum of Natural History." His first exhibit was the skull of a seal from the fish market.

Working Out

When Teedie was eleven, his father had a gym built on the second-floor porch and challenged Teedie to build up his frail body. Teedie couldn't ignore a challenge. He spent long hours lifting weights, swinging from the horizontal bars, pounding the punching bag.

It was hard work. But Teedie had a way of finding the fun in things. One day, his mother was horrified to see Teedie and his cousin balancing the seesaw board on the porch railing. Teedie

Family legend says that, at the age of eleven, Teedie declared, "I'll make my body!"

hung out in midair, two stories up.

As Teedie grew older, his family began spending summers at the ocean. The fresh air agreed with him. He still had bouts of asthma. But he eagerly went rowing and horseback riding and exploring.

A NEW WORLD

He'd kept his love of nature. Unfortunately he'd been taught that to study animals, you had to kill them. His father gave him his first gun when he was thirteen. When he took it hunting, though, he found that "my companions seemed to see things to shoot at which I could not see at all." A doctor examined his eyes and fitted him with thick spectacles.

The glasses "opened an entirely new world" to him. They also gave other boys a new reason to make fun of him. They'd always called him a sissy and a weakling. Now they called him "Four Eyes" too. His brother Elliott had always stood up for him. But on a trip to Maine, Teedie was stuck in a stagecoach with two big boys his own age. They tormented him the whole way. Instead of feeling sorry for himself, Teedie grew even more determined to build himself up.

A sketch by the young naturalist of one of his "specimens"—perhaps the same mouse he preserved in the family's icebox

TEDDY

He was also determined to go to college. But he had to make up for all the schooling he'd missed. For two years, he studied six to eight hours a day. Then he was accepted at Harvard College.

Harvard was full of young men from rich families. But Teddy, as he now called himself, didn't fit in. The typical "Harvard Man" pretended not to care about anything, even schoolwork. Teddy was enthusiastic about everything. Instead of strolling, he ran. Instead of looking bored, he showed his large teeth in a grin that became his trademark. Instead of drawling, he poured out his words in a loud, high-pitched voice. Instead of sleeping through classes, he argued with the teachers.

During Teddy's second year at Harvard, his father fell ill with cancer. The family sent for Teddy. By the time he arrived, his father was dead.

A NEW CAREER
Numb with grief, Teddy buried himself in his books. But he loved life too much

Teddy as a "Harvard Man." Note the fashionable "muttonchop" whiskers.

to stay buried long. He took up sports; he went to parties; he joined clubs and societies. By his senior year, he was one of the most popular students. Instead of changing himself, Teddy had changed the way his classmates saw him. They no longer considered him a fool. They knew he was just different.

He did change in one way, though. "I fully intended to make science my life work," he wrote. Now he'd given up those plans. The reason was a bright, pretty girl named Alice Lee. He met her in his junior year and immediately fell in love. Like most people, Alice was overwhelmed by his enthusiastic manner. But Teddy didn't mind; he tried all the harder to win her. It took him more than a year, but he finally convinced Alice to marry him.

Alice's family was rich and well known. They might welcome a lawyer or a banker into the family, but not an ordinary scientist. Teddy didn't really need a career. His father had left him plenty of money. But he wasn't the sort to sit idle.

Doctors had warned him that he had a weak heart and shouldn't strain himself. Teddy felt that a short, active life was better than a long, inactive one. "Life is a great adventure," he said, "and the worst of all fears is the fear of living."

He looked for a new challenge and found it in politics. He started by winning a seat in the New York Assembly in 1881. At twenty-three, he was the youngest man there. He didn't fit in any better than he had at Harvard. But in time he won everyone over.

Ever since he'd read Mayne Reid's

Tall, graceful Alice Lee had lots of admirers, but none quite like Teddy.

In his early days in the Dakota Badlands, Teddy dressed like a "dude." But he proved himself as tough as any real cowboy.

novels, Teddy had been fascinated by the West. In 1883, he went to the Dakota Territory on a buffalo hunt. When he returned, he had not only bagged a buffalo, he'd invested half his money in a cattle ranch.

One day, back at the state capital, Teddy got a telegram saying he was the father of a baby girl. A few hours later, a second telegram came. His wife, Alice, was very weak from the birth. Teddy's mother was sick, too, with typhoid fever.

Remembering his father's death, Teddy rushed home. There was nothing he or the doctors could do. His mother died the next morning. Eleven hours later Alice died, too, in his arms. Teddy wrote, "The light went from my life forever."

He managed to finish his term in the assembly. Then, leaving "Baby Lee" with his sister Anna, he retreated to his cattle ranch. "It was still the Wild West in those days," he wrote, "a land of scattered ranches, of herds of long-horned cattle, and of reckless riders." He hoped that the rough life of a cowboy would make him forget his grief.

It did much more than that. It shaped the rest of his life.

THEODORE

Teddy the cattle rancher was now calling himself Theodore. But otherwise he hadn't changed much. He was still scrawny and weak, and still had stomach and lung problems. He had the same squeaky voice, the same toothy grin, the same thick glasses. And, though he was shaken by the death of his wife, he had the same great enthusiasm for life.

Behind his back, the real cowboys laughed at the "dude." Theodore didn't care. He loved the West. He wrote, "I do not believe there was ever any life more attractive to a vigorous young fellow than life on a cattle ranch."

Theodore put a lot more than his money into the ranch. He worked as hard as any cowhand. He rode wild horses; he fought prairie fires; he "beavered down" logs to build a new ranch house. In the evenings he went on working at his desk, writing books and articles.

LAW AND ORDER

His hard work won the respect of the

cowboys. But two incidents made him a legend in Dakota. The first happened when he was trailing a band of horses. He stopped for the night at a small hotel. A "shabby individual in a broad hat" came up with pistols drawn and said that "Four Eyes" was going to buy drinks for everyone. Theodore shrugged and got to his feet, as if he meant to do it. Instead, he delivered two punches to the man's jaw. The troublemaker toppled to the floor. Theodore calmly took away the man's guns.

Theodore admired the untamed way of life out West. But he also believed in

Theodore the hunter. Actually, this picture was taken to promote one of Theodore's books. The buckskin suit is real; the studio setting isn't.

law and order. He soon got a chance to prove it. One day, three horse thieves were escaping down the Little Missouri River in a leaky boat. When they came to the Elkhorn, Theodore's ranch, they stole his boat.

The weather was bitterly cold, and the outlaws had a big head start. Most men would have let them go. But not Theodore. His men quickly built a new boat and, with two men, Theodore set off after the thieves.

After three days, he caught them. He took their weapons and boots, and the group spent six miserable days struggling down the ice-choked river.

Finally they reached a ranch. Theodore hired a wagon and driver. He let the thieves ride. He walked behind, guarding them. Two days and forty miles later, grimy, blistered, and exhausted, he turned them over to the sheriff. People asked why he hadn't just hanged them. Theodore wanted to do things the civilized way.

THE END OF THE TRAIL

He made ranch life more civilized, too. He bought a rubber bathtub to soak in. He insisted on having milk to drink, even though it meant having to "race a cow two miles at full speed . . . rope her, throw her, and turn her upside down."

As much as he loved the ranch, he was restless. Every few months he took the train back East to see his daughter. He also began seeing a friend from his childhood, Edith Carow. Now they were more than friends. Though he felt he was being untrue to Alice, he asked

Edith to marry him. They were married in December 1886.

That winter, while Theodore was in New York, Dakota was hit by the worst blizzard in history. When the snow melted in the spring, the prairie was a vast graveyard of dead cows.

It was the end of Theodore's career as a rancher. He'd spent less than two years in the West, but the experience had left its mark on him. As usual, he'd changed how people saw him. But this time Theodore had changed, too. Thanks to the active life, he'd put on thirty pounds of muscle, and his health was good at last. He was more sure of himself and his abilities. He was a man of action now, not of dreams.

"I owe more than I can ever express to the West," he wrote. He never forgot

Edith Carow, a childhood friend, became Theodore's second wife, then the nation's First Lady.

Theodore and friends stand before a giant sequoia tree. Roosevelt's Boone and Crockett Club helped create the National Forest system.

it. When he became president, he set aside public lands in the West, to protect them. He saw that dams were built to provide water so that crops could grow on land that once supported only cattle.

After he left Dakota, it took Theodore only fourteen years to become president. Into those fourteen years he packed a lifetime of experiences.

THE COLONEL

In 1886, Theodore had run for mayor of New York City and lost. He felt his future in politics was over. He decided to make writing his career. He'd already published several popular books about his life out West. Now Theodore began an ambitious history, *The Winning of the West*. The first volumes got good reviews and sold well.

But politics, like his asthma, kept re-entering his life. In 1889, Theodore's old friends got him a position as a Civil Service commissioner. As usual, Theodore wasn't content to do things as they'd always been done. The Civil Service is in charge of hiring people for government jobs. In the past, those jobs had gone to people in return for favors. Theodore insisted that they go to the people who could do them best. His reforms made him a lot of enemies.

But they also made him well known, and led to his next position: police commissioner of New York City. Once again, Theodore shook things up. He fired the police superintendent, started an

New York City Police Commissioner Roosevelt in his office

academy to train policemen, and promoted only those who were honest and hardworking.

Late at night, he roamed the streets of the city, checking up on his men. He became such a familiar figure that the street peddlers began selling whistles in the shape of "Teddy's Teeth."

PREPARING FOR WAR

Theodore's image as a reformer bothered more cautious politicians. When William McKinley became president in 1897, Theodore wanted to be his assistant secretary of the navy. But McKinley hesitated. He thought Theodore was "hot-headed and harum-scarum." The secretary of the navy was afraid Theodore would try to take over his department.

He was right. Theodore got the job anyway, and immediately set about changing things. He knew the United States would fight a war sooner or later, and he wanted the navy to be ready. He turned up unexpectedly to inspect ships. Because of Theodore's reputation for getting things done, anyone who had a problem waited until the secretary wasn't around and talked to him instead.

Theodore's warnings about a war soon proved correct. Americans had long felt that European countries had no business running things in North and South America. But Spain ruled the island of Cuba, and that made the United States government nervous. The United States wanted to control the Caribbean and planned to build a canal linking it with the Pacific Ocean.

The Cubans wanted the Spanish out, too. Early in 1898, fighting broke out. Theodore sent the battleship *Maine* to protect Americans on the island. On February 15, the *Maine* exploded, killing most of its crew. It was probably an accident, but Americans blamed the Spanish. Theodore ordered the navy to prepare for war.

THE ROUGH RIDERS

When war came, Theodore was nearly forty. But he wasn't content to sit behind a desk. He resigned and got permission to form a regiment of volunteer soldiers, the First U.S. Volunteer Cavalry.

$50,000 REWARD.—WHO DESTROYED THE MAINE?—$50,000 REWARD.

EDITION FOR GREATER NEW YORK

NEW YORK JOURNAL
AND ADVERTISER.

NEW YORK, THURSDAY, FEBRUARY 17, 1898.—16 PAGES.   PRICE ONE CENT

DESTRUCTION OF THE WAR SHIP MAINE WAS THE WORK OF AN ENEMY.

$50,000!

$50,000 REWARD!
For the Detection of the
Perpetrator of
the Maine Outrage!

Assistant Secretary Roosevelt Convinced the Explosion of the War Ship Was Not an Accident.

The Journal Offers $50,000 Reward for the Conviction of the Criminals Who Sent 258 American Sailors to Their Death. Naval Officers Unanimous That the Ship Was Destroyed on Purpose.

$50,000!

$50,000 REWARD!
For the Detection of the
Perpetrator of
the Maine Outrage!

No one knows for certain what caused the battleship Maine *to explode, but "Remember the Maine!" became the battle cry in the war against Spain.*

They were a strange lot: classmates from Harvard and cowboys from Dakota; buffalo hunters and Texas Rangers; Native Americans and old Indian fighters; men with names like Happy Jack and Rattlesnake Pete and Prayerful James.

Their mascots were just as strange: a mongrel dog named Cuba, a moody mountain lion named Josephine, and an eagle. The three constantly tormented one another.

But the men got along amazingly well. They were known at first as Teddy's Terrors, then as the Rough Riders. Tired of waiting for action, Theodore took over a ship meant for

A sketch of Colonel Roosevelt in his Rough Rider uniform, by a famous illustrator of the time, Charles Dana Gibson

another regiment. He and his men set sail for Cuba, chanting:

> Rough, rough, we're the stuff!
> We want to fight, and we can't get enough!
> Whoopee!

UNDER FIRE

They landed at the port of Daiquiri and headed for the Spanish-held city of Santiago. Although they were cavalry, only the officers had horses. They pushed through "mountainous country covered with thick jungle," sweating and swatting mosquitoes. A week later, they were at the foot of a range of hills topped by houses made into forts.

The Spanish opened fire and began picking off Theodore's men one by one. Theodore leaped onto his horse, Texas, and gave the order to charge. Halfway up the hill, he hit a wire fence and had to leave his horse behind. Bullets whizzed by with "a sound like the ripping of a silk dress." Eighty-six of the Rough Riders were killed or wounded. Theodore came through with only a scratch. Once they took the hill, they were still under fire from San Juan Hill, to their left. Some of the men took cover behind a huge iron kettle, which gave the hill its name: Kettle Hill.

Never one to sit still, Theodore led a second charge toward "a line of hills farther on." He got a hundred yards before he realized that only four men were with him. He scrambled back and collected the others, who hadn't heard his order.

Newspapers called Theodore the "Hero of San Juan Hill." He was recommended

This painting depicting the Charge of San Juan Hill is more fanciful than factual. Most of the Rough Riders wore flannel shirts and sombreros, and they charged the hill on foot.

for a Medal of Honor, but his political enemies made sure he didn't get it. They also pointed out that he hadn't actually gone up San Juan Hill. Theodore replied, "We certainly charged some hills; but I did not ask their names before charging them."

THE HERO

Nothing his enemies said mattered to the American people. To them, "The Colonel" was a hero, the sort Theodore had once admired in books. He took advantage of his popularity by running for governor of New York State, and won. Naturally, he wasted no time in reforming things and upsetting people. But the public loved him and his goal of honest government.

When McKinley ran again in 1900, he was urged to choose "The Colonel" as vice president. But McKinley wanted someone "safe." Theodore didn't want the job, either. It wasn't enough of a challenge.

But he was so popular that he was nominated anyway. He traveled all over the country, speaking with such energy that people thought he was the one running for president. Those speeches did a lot to help McKinley win.

As Theodore expected, he didn't have much to do as vice president. He did spend more time with his family. He had five children now, and he loved their company. In fact, he often behaved like one of them. They played hide-and-seek, told ghost stories, and took "obstacle walks" across the countryside.

Still, Theodore was restless. He took any offer to speak, just to be doing something. In September 1901, he was

Roosevelt's dramatic and enthusiastic speaking style won a lot of votes, first for President McKinley, then for himself.

Roosevelt plays ball with his children and their friends at the "summer White House" at Sagamore Hill.

speaking in northern New York when word came that the president had been shot while on a visit to Buffalo. Theodore rushed there, but doctors had removed the bullets, and McKinley seemed to be out of danger. Theodore joined his family in the Adirondack Mountains. Three days later, he got word that McKinley was dead. That meant Theodore was president.

MR. PRESIDENT

Theodore faced his biggest challenge—running the country. He delighted in it. This time he was smart enough not to upset things, at least not right away. He followed McKinley's lead for a while.

But it wasn't long before he went where no president had gone before. He was the first president to fly in an airplane, the first to go down in a submarine, the first to travel outside the United States while in office.

When coal miners walked off their jobs, demanding more pay, it created a major coal shortage. Schools closed. Mobs seized coal cars. Peopled chopped down telegraph poles for firewood. Theodore brought the miners and their managers together and told them to work it out, or he'd send in troops to run the mines. They worked it out.

PART OF THE WORLD

He used this same method time and again to solve problems: Make a reasonable offer, but back it up with a threat of force. Or, as Theodore put it, quoting an old African saying, "Speak softly, and carry a big stick."

He didn't use his big stick only at home. Unlike other presidents, he saw the United States not as an isolated country, but as part of the world. He settled a war between Russia and Japan the same way he'd settled the miners' strike. He brought the two sides together and insisted they make peace. They did. For his efforts, Theodore was given the Nobel Peace Prize, the first Nobel Prize won by an American.

One of his biggest "sticks" was the navy. He made it the second strongest in the world. To prove it, he sent sixty battleships on a voyage around the globe, the first time that had been done.

"I have been able to do much that

Theodore was a favorite subject of political cartoonists, who often pictured him clobbering wrongdoers with his "big stick."

Theodore with naturalist John Muir at Yosemite National Park. During Roosevelt's presidency, five new national parks were created.

was worth doing," he wrote. Of all the things he accomplished, two seemed most important to him. One was setting aside national parks and forests for public use. The other was building the Panama Canal, which connected the Caribbean Sea with the Pacific Ocean.

The public liked the things he did, and they loved the man himself. They loved his bigger-than-life personality and the great delight he took in everything. When he was made an honorary member of a Native American tribe, he led a whooping war dance around the Oval Office. He invited colorful characters to the White House, including cowboys and Rough Riders. He did ask them to leave their guns at home. He shocked people by having an African American, Booker T. Washington, as a dinner guest.

The White House had its own police force, and Theodore's sons, Archie and Quentin, liked to join its ranks.

The Roosevelt family became celebrities, like today's movie stars. Newspapers followed their every move. On a bear hunt in Mississippi, Theodore's guides tracked down a young black bear and tied it up. But Theodore refused to shoot a captive bear. Newspapers all over the country printed the story. It inspired a toy maker to create a cuddly stuffed bear that became the favorite of millions of children—the teddy bear.

A REAL PRESIDENT

Despite Theodore's popularity, somewhere inside he was still the weak,

A 1903 portrait of the First Family. Theodore and Edith with the children (from the left): *Quentin, aged five; Ted, fifteen; Archie, nine; Alice, nineteen; Kermit, thirteen; and Ethel, eleven.*

When teddy bears became wildly popular across the country, cartoonists began portraying the Roosevelts as a family of lively bears.

Theodore believed in letting the voters see and hear him, and he traveled thousands of miles by train to make sure that they did.

sickly Teedie who had to prove himself. He knew he had become president only through McKinley's death. He wondered if he could really win an election on his own.

In 1904, he did, by more votes than any president in history. He would surely have been reelected in 1908. But he felt no president should serve more than two terms.

Four years later, disappointed with President Taft, he changed his mind and ran again. While he was speaking in Milwaukee, a mentally ill man shot him. The bullet struck his glasses case, tore through the copy of his speech, and dug into his ribs. Ignoring the wound, he went on to speak for an hour and a half.

Because three men were running for president, the vote was split up, and

Woodrow Wilson won. Theodore didn't sit around moping. Instead he went to Brazil, to help map a wild, unexplored river. For weeks, his party hacked through dense jungle and fought rapids. Theodore injured a leg, then fell ill with malaria. He had to be carried the rest of the way.

A Quiet End

His health was never good again after that. But it didn't slow him down. When the United States entered World War I in 1917, he was fifty-nine. He was blind in one eye from a boxing injury; his leg pained him; he was weak from malaria. Still, he wanted to raise a new company of Rough Riders. He was turned down.

Theodore thought seriously of running for president in 1920. But, though his

Theodore's larger-than-life image made him a celebrity around the world.

To his grandchildren, Theodore wasn't Mr. President—just a doting grandfather.

spirit was strong, his body was worn out. On January 6, 1919, he died—not, as he had always expected, on a battlefield, or hunting a lion or grizzly, but quietly in his own bed.

His sister Corinne later wrote that he would have liked to have died for his country. Instead, he lived for it.

Glossary

assassin: A murderer, usually one who kills a well-known person, often for political reasons.

asthma (AZ-muh): A lung problem, sometimes caused by allergies. The bronchial tubes (which bring air to the lungs) shrink, making it hard to breathe.

battleship: A large ship with a heavy metal hull. It is designed to travel fast, and is armed with huge guns.

blizzard: A strong, freezing wind with blowing snow.

Caribbean Sea: A warm part of the Atlantic Ocean between North and South America. It contains many islands, including Cuba, Puerto Rico, and Jamaica.

cavalry: A branch of the army that fought battles on horseback. During the war in Cuba, only the officers rode horses.

Civil Service: The branch of government in charge of hiring people for certain government jobs.

Dakota Territory: The area of the West that is now the states of North Dakota and South Dakota.

drawling: Talking slowly and lazily.

Harvard College: Part of Harvard University in Cambridge, Massachusetts. The oldest college in the United States.

harum-scarum: Reckless or irresponsible.

hedgehog: Another name for a porcupine. True hedgehogs live in Europe and aren't related to porcupines.

malaria: A disease common in tropical climates. The victim suffers from a high fever, then from chills. Humans get malaria from the bite of a mosquito.

mongrel: A mutt; a dog of no particular breed.

nominated: Every four years members of the big political parties choose, or *nominate*, a person to run for president and one to run for vice president.

Panama Canal: A "big ditch" dug across the narrow country of Panama in Central America. The waterway lets ships pass from the Caribbean Sea to the Pacific Ocean. Before it was dug, ships had to sail thousands of miles around the tip of South America to get to the Pacific.

reformer: A man or woman who tries to have laws passed that will improve people's lives or get rid of injustices.

trademark: A word or symbol that identifies a product; also used to mean a special trait or physical feature that sets a person apart from others.

typhoid (TIE-foid) **fever:** An illness caused by bacteria found in dirty water or food. In Theodore Roosevelt's day, a third of the people who caught typhoid fever died from it.

To Learn More About Theodore Roosevelt

Books

Fritz, Jean. *Bully for You, Teddy Roosevelt.* New York: Putnam, 1991. A brief, readable biography with striking black-and-white illustrations.

McCafferty, Jim. *Holt and the Teddy Bear.* Gretna, LA: Pelican Publishing, 1991. A fictional account of the famous bear incident, with color illustrations.

Monjo, F. N. *The One Bad Thing about Father.* New York: Harper, 1970. Easy reader. Theodore's presidency and life in the White House, as told through the eyes of his son Quentin.

Quackenbush, Robert. *Don't You Dare Shoot That Bear!: A Story of Theodore Roosevelt.* Englewood Cliffs, NJ: Prentice-Hall, 1984. Not just about the bear. A humorous but accurate account of Theodore's life.

Singer, A. L. *The Young Indiana Jones Chronicles: Safari Sleuth.* New York: Random House, 1992. Based on the TV series. A fictional adventure in which young Indy meets Teddy on a big-game hunt in Africa.

Whitelaw, Nancy. *Theodore Roosevelt Takes Charge*. Morton Grove, IL: Whitman, 1992. A long and complete biography, with lots of photographs.

Videos

A Walk Through the Twentieth Century with Bill Moyers: TR and His Times. Alexandria, VA: PBS Video, 1988. A one-hour video that's often entertaining and has some rare film footage of Theodore in action.

Museums

Theodore Roosevelt Birthplace National Historic Site. 28 East 20th Street, New York City. Theodore's boyhood home with period furnishings. Open Wednesday–Sunday.

Sagamore Hill National Historic Site. Oyster Bay, Long Island, New York. Theodore's family home and summer White House. Original furnishings and historic items. Open April–September.

Theodore Roosevelt Memorial Bird Sanctuary and Trailside Museum. Oyster Bay, Long Island, New York. Trails and displays. Theodore's grave is nearby, in Young's Cemetery.

Theodore Roosevelt National Park. Medora, South Dakota. 70,000-acre park with visitor center. Theodore's Maltese Cross and Elkhorn ranch houses. In the nearby town of Medora are historic buildings including the Rough Riders Hotel, a store owned by Theodore's partner.

Index

Page numbers for illustrations are in boldface.

Notes

The quotations in this book are from the following sources:

Page 7, "nobody seemed to think": interview in *New York World*, quoted in *Mornings on Horseback* by David McCullough, p. 95.

Page 8, "He was everything": *Personal Diaries*, quoted in *That Damned Cowboy: Theodore Roosevelt and the American West, 1883–1898* by Michael L. Collins, p. 10.

Page 10, "hedgehogs": *An Autobiography* by Theodore Roosevelt, p. 20.

Page 11, "my companions" and "opened an entirely new world": *Autobiography*, p. 18.

Page 14, "I fully intended": *Autobiography*, p. 24.

Page 15, "Life is a great adventure": *Autobiography*, p. 347.

Page 17, "The light went": "In Memory of My Darling Wife," quoted in *That Damned Cowboy*, p. 3.

Page 17, "It was still the Wild West": *Autobiography*, p. 93.

Page 18, "I do not believe": *Autobiography*, p. 95.

Page 18, "beavered down": *Autobiography*, p. 97.

Page 19, "shabby individual": *Autobiography*, p. 122.

Page 20, "race a cow": *Autobiography*, p. 96.

Page 21, "I owe more": *Autobiography*, p. 119.

Page 25, "hot-headed": *Letters*, vol 1, quoted in *Theodore Roosevelt: A Life* by Nathan Miller, p. 246.

Page 28, "mountainous country": *Autobiography*, p. 236.

Page 28, "a sound like": *Autobiography*, p. 237.

Page 28, "a line of hills": *Autobiography*, p. 243.

Page 30, "We certainly charged": *Autobiography*, p. 257.

Pages 35-36, "I have been able": Letter quoted in *My Brother, Theodore Roosevelt* by Corinne Roosevelt Robinson, p. 217.

ABOUT THE AUTHOR

Gary L. Blackwood is the author of several fiction books for young readers, including *Wild Timothy* and *Beyond the Door*. His interest in Theodore Roosevelt began when he was doing research for a novel about Theodore's years as a cattle rancher in Dakota.

Gary also writes plays, sometimes about historical characters like Belle Starr. He lives with his wife and two children in the Missouri town where Belle Starr grew up. Like Theodore, he and his family are fond of nature and love animals; unlike Theodore, they prefer not to shoot or eat them.